Cathedral
Window

The Classic QUILT Series #5

LAURA NOWNES

The Quilt Digest Press

Project direction by Michael Kile.
Editorial direction by Harold Nadel.
Book and cover design by Kajun Graphics.
Quilt, cover and room setting photographs by
Sharon Risedorph.
Computer graphics by Kandy Petersen.
Typographical composition by DC Typography.
Printed by Nissha Printing Company, Ltd., Kyoto, Japan.
Color separations by the printer.
Home graciously lent by Ronnie Gilbert and Donna
Korones.
Special thanks to Margaret Stephenson Coole.

For Adele, with many thanks for her continued help.

First Printing.

Library of Congress Cataloging-in-Publication Data

Nownes, Laura, 1953-
    Cathedral window / Laura Nownes.
       p.   cm. – (The classic quilt series : #5)
    ISBN 0-913327-27-1 (ppr) : $6.95
    1. Patchwork–Patterns. 2. Quilting–Patterns. I. Title.
  II. Series : Nownes, Laura, 1953- Classic quilt series : #5.
  TT835.N679 1991
  746.9'7– dc20   90-28956
                                     CIP

The Quilt Digest Press
P.O. Box 1331
Gualala, CA 95445

INTRODUCTION

Cathedral Window is a favorite among classic quilt techniques. Its fascinating texture allows you to utilize a wide range of fabric and color choices. The construction is easy enough for a novice quiltmaker, but the possibilities are varied enough to stimulate the creative imagination of a lifelong quiltmaker.

You will note that the amount of *Background* fabric required is considerably more than you are accustomed to buying for a background: this quilt has no separate backing or batting layer. The background fabric is folded and stitched to four thicknesses, in square units, to create a heavily textured framework of cloth; the units are then joined together to form the quilt. The easy construction presented here was developed and generously shared by Adele Ingraham.

Pieces of fabric called *Windows* are placed over the seams joining the units. The windows are held in place by frames of background fabric which are folded and stitched over their edges.

An optional piece of fabric, called an *Accent*, can also be inserted into the folded background unit before the window is added. This accent fabric adds yet another set of colors and another dimension to the quilt.

A variation on the traditional square *Cathedral Window* unit is a rectangular unit which produces a diamond-shaped window. I include this variation because it increases your design possibilities endlessly. When you combine rectangular units with square ones, you will create unusual patterns and optical illusions. For her generous sharing of her designs, we are all indebted to Margaret Stephenson Coole.

Besides the possibilities offered for planned color arrangements in the background, windows and accents, you will discover that *Cathedral Window* is a perfect opportunity for using up a wide selection of small scraps.

I include here a variety of *Cathedral Window* quilts. Set your imagination loose and make one today!

Happy quilting!

Laura

Laura Nownes

WHAT YOU NEED

Fabric:

Background: This fabric will show on both the front and backside of your quilt, so it is important to use a good quality. Since the fabric is folded to four thicknesses, it becomes very heavy. Avoid using too thick or heavy a fabric. A medium-weight stable fabric works best. If it is too thin, the units may stretch out of shape.

Windows: Since the window pieces simply lie flat over the seams, almost any fabric can be used, from light-weight silk to heavy velveteen. If your window fabric is too thin or sheer, you may want to use two thicknesses to prevent a darker background fabric from showing through.

Accent: A medium-weight stable fabric. Avoid too thick or heavy a fabric, as the edges are turned under and stitched.

Pre-wash and press your fabric in preparation for cutting.

Rotary cutter, wide plastic ruler and cutting board, or fabric scissors

Glass-head pins

Good-quality thread in a color to match the background fabric

Hand sewing needle (Sharp or Between)

Small embroidery scissors

Steam iron

Light-colored towel

Pressing surface

Sewing machine (optional)

MAKING YOUR QUILT

The *Cathedral Window* pattern can be constructed either entirely by hand or partially by machine and finished by hand. My preference is to use the machine for Steps 1-17 and complete the construction by hand. I love handwork and I find it easier to achieve neat, tight intersections by hand than by machine. If you enjoy machine work, I encourage you to experiment with joining your squares together by machine. It is certainly a timesaver and, with a little practice, you can achieve neat results. The armchair caddy on page 20, which requires only four square units, is a perfect project for working on the techniques.

SQUARE UNITS

1. Cut a square of background fabric the required size for the desired finished size you wish to make.

Step 3

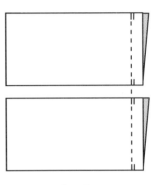
Step 4

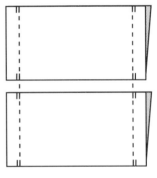
Step 6

Step 8

Refer to the cutting charts for the individual quilts. Cutting squares may seem a simple task; however, it is important that they be *perfectly* square, following the grainline of the fabric; otherwise, the entire quilt will become distorted.

Since you will be working with many yards of fabric, it will be easier to cut the entire piece into shorter lengths. First, fold your fabric in half lengthwise, selvage edges even with each other. Then make a straight lengthwise cut along the fabric to remove the selvage edges. Measure over from this newly cut edge to make lengthwise strips the required size of your squares. Next, cut the strips into squares along the crossgrain. Double check to see that your cuts are along the crosswise threads of the fabric.

Place your squares in stacks near your sewing machine, with their lengthwise grain all going in the same direction. If you are using a fabric which has definite wrong and right sides, you will want the right side facing up. Some fabrics will appear to be slightly different colors and/or textures when viewed lengthwise or crosswise. For this reason, it is best to keep your squares all facing the same direction.

2. Pick up the top square of background fabric and fold it in half with the wrong side facing out.

3. Beginning and ending with a few backstitches, stitch along one side of the folded square with a ¼" seam, stitching from the cut edges to the fold, as shown.

If you are hand sewing, thread your needle with a single strand of thread without a knot at the end. Begin and end with two small backstitches and sew with small running stitches.

4. If you are using a sewing machine for this step, do not remove the square from your machine; instead, feed another folded square into the machine and sew along one side in the same manner, as shown. Do not cut the chain of thread holding the two squares together.

5. Continue stitching along one side of the remaining squares, either by hand or by feeding them successively through the machine. Do not cut the chain of thread holding the squares together if you are using a sewing machine.

6. Next, stitch all of the folded squares along each opposite side, as shown.

7. If you used a sewing machine, cut the threads joining the fabric pieces.

8. Use your scissors to trim the bottom folded corners of each fabric piece, at an angle similar to the one shown.

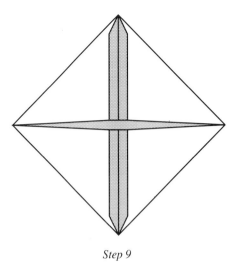

Step 9

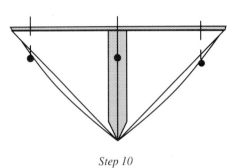

Step 10

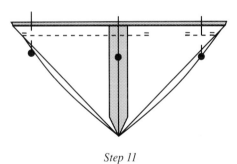

Step 11

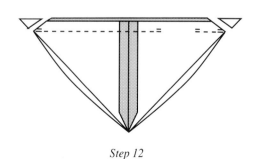

Step 12

9. Fold the fabric piece, as shown. Then run your thumbnail firmly along the seams to open them flat.

10. With right sides together and unsewn raw edges even, position the opened seams back to back and secure them with a pin. Place two more pins at opposite ends, as shown.

11. Stitch the unsewn raw edges together, beginning and ending with a few backstitches and leaving a 1½″ opening, as shown.

12. Use your scissors to trim the two top corners of each fabric piece, at an angle similar to the one shown.

13. Lay the fabric piece out flat so that the seams are facing up. Then carefully run the tip of your iron along the seams to open them flat.

14. Carefully turn the square right side out through the 1½″ opening left in Step 11. You may want to use the tip end of a small pair of scissors to push the corners out carefully to a sharp point.

15. With the seamed side facing up, firmly press the fabric square (which is now two thicknesses) flat onto a pressing surface which has been covered with a light-colored towel. The seams should end sharply at each corner point.

16. Bring the corner points to the centerpoint and secure with pins inserted vertically into the pressing surface at the centerpoint and corners, as shown.

17. Spray water lightly onto the square to dampen. Then use a steam iron and apply pressure to make sharp corner points and create creases where the fabric has been folded. Let cool. Remove the pins.

If you have been using a machine, continue working through Steps 18-25. If you have been hand sewing, proceed to the section "Finishing By Hand."

18. To join squares: with their seam lines facing out, place two fabric squares together and stitch them along the creased lines, as shown. If the 1½″ opening is always placed in the same position when joining squares, grainline will automatically be consistent.

19. In the same manner, unfold the squares and stitch another square to one of them. Continue, to form a row.

20. With their seam lines facing out, place two rows backsides together and stitch lengthwise along the folded lines, from square to square, as shown.

21. Attach additional rows as required.

This quilt can quickly become very heavy and awkward to work with. You may want to work on small sections at a time. Later, join the sections to complete the quilt.

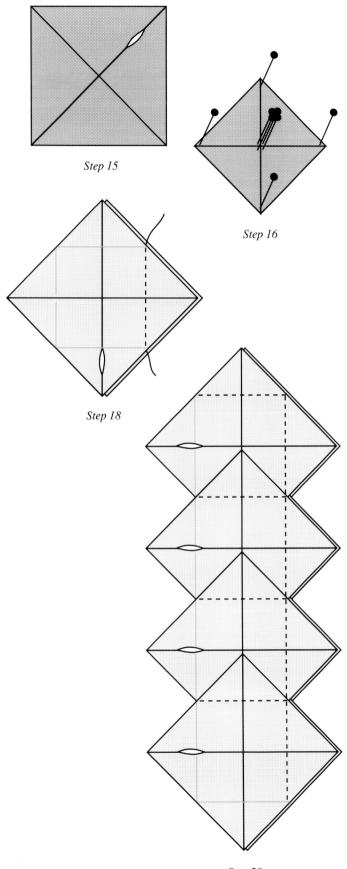

Step 15

Step 16

Step 18

Step 20

If you want to add an inlay of accent fabric, this is the point at which it is attached. See the instructions under "Variation" below for help. Then proceed with Steps 22-25.

22. Use your needle and thread to hand tack the loose corners to the centerpoint of each square. Your stitches should go all the way through to the backside of the fabric. If you are working in small sections, do not tack those triangles which will later be joined to other sections.

23. With its right side facing up, center a piece of window fabric over *each* seam line joining two squares, as shown. Secure them with pins.

24. Turn one loose side of the background fabric square over the raw edge of the window fabric and hand stitch it in place. Stitch only through the two top layers of background fabric.

To keep the corners of the windows neat, stitch to within approximately ⅜″ of a corner. Working clockwise, fold the next loose side over the window fabric and hold it in place. Then take two small stitches to join these sides and pull to hold secure. If you wish, slip stitch the folded edges together up to the point. Run the needle and thread through the folded edge and bring it out at the point where the two small holding stitches were made. Continue sewing. Repeat.

25. When all of the window fabrics have been stitched in place and all sections joined, the quilt is complete — no batting, no separate backing or binding.

FINISHING BY HAND

If you want to add an inlay of accent fabric, this is the point at which it is attached. See the instructions under "Variation" below for help. Then proceed with Steps 1-7.

1. Use your needle and thread to hand tack the loose corners to the centerpoint of each square. Your stitches should go all the way through to the backside of the fabric.

2. To join squares: with their backsides facing each other, place two squares together, their edges even. Use a small hand whip stitch, catching just the top edges of the fabric to join two squares together, as shown. Small ridges of stitches will form on the right side of the quilt; however, they will be covered over with the window fabrics.

3. Stitch more fabric squares together in the same manner to form a row of squares.

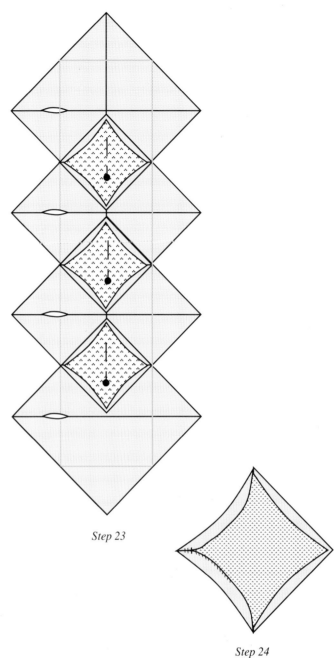

Step 23

Step 24

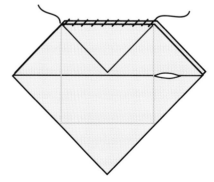

Finishing by hand
Step 2

4. Place two rows backsides facing each other and stitch lengthwise in the same manner as instructed in Step 2.

5. Attach additional rows as required.

6. Insert window fabrics over each seam line joining two squares. Refer to Steps 23 and 24 above for instructions.

7. When all of the window fabrics have been stitched in place, the quilt is complete — no batting, no separate backing or binding.

VARIATION: INLAY OF ACCENT FABRIC

An example of this variation is used on the armchair caddy. You can use it on any of your *Cathedral Window* quilts.

1. Cut the required number of accent pieces. The cut size is the finished size of your unit plus ¼" allowance on all sides. For example, for a 4" finished square unit, cut a 4½" square of accent fabric.

2. With the wrong side facing up, lay an accent piece on the pressing surface. Turn the edges in ¼" and press.

3. With its right side facing up, center an accent piece over a background square, as shown.

4. Hand tack it in place around the edges, stitching only through the top layer of background fabric. Since the stitches near the corners will show in the finished quilt, now is the time to be neat!

5. Now, complete Steps 22-25 of "Square Units" to finish your *Cathedral Window*.

RECTANGULAR UNITS

As you can see by looking at the template patterns for the rectangular units, these shapes cannot be cut using quick-cutting techniques; you must make a template of the shape. Notice that in some cases only a portion of the entire shape is given. Make a full-size template and then use it for marking the shape onto your fabric. You can layer your fabric and cut several thicknesses at once to save time. Basic construction of the rectangular unit is similar to that of the square unit.

1. Use the appropriate template pattern to cut the background fabric shapes for the quilt you are making.

2. With their right sides facing up, place the fabric shapes in a stack, positioned as shown.

3. Pick up the top fabric piece and fold it in half with the wrong side facing out, as shown.

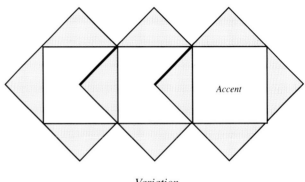

Variation
Step 3

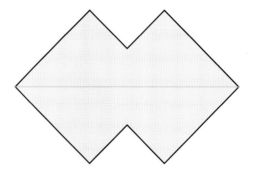

Rectangular Units
Step 2

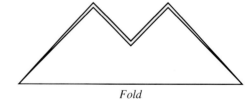

Fold

Step 3

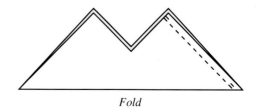

Fold

Step 4

4. Beginning and ending with a few backstitches, stitch along one side of the folded fabric piece with a ¼″ seam, stitching from the cut edges to the fold, as shown.

If you are hand sewing, thread your needle with a single strand of thread without a knot at the end. Begin and end with two small backstitches and sew with small running stitches.

5. If you are using a sewing machine for this step, do not remove the fabric piece from your machine; instead, feed another folded fabric piece into the machine and sew along one side in the same manner. Do not cut the chain of thread holding the pieces together.

6. Next, stitch all of the folded fabric pieces along each opposite side, leaving a 1½″ opening, beginning and ending with a few backstitches, as shown.

7. If you used a sewing machine, cut the threads joining fabric pieces.

8. Use your scissors to trim the bottom folded corners of each fabric piece, at an angle similar to the one shown.

9. Fold the fabric piece as shown. Then run your thumbnail firmly along the seams to open them flat.

10. With right sides together and unsewn raw edges even, position the opened seams back to back and secure them with a pin. Place two more pins at opposite ends, as shown.

11. Stitch the unsewn raw edges together, beginning and ending with a few backstitches, as shown.

12. See Steps 13 through 25 of "Square Units" for finishing the rectangular units, inserting the diamond window pieces and joining the units to complete the quilt.

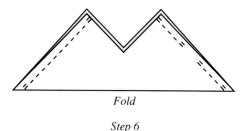

Fold

Step 6

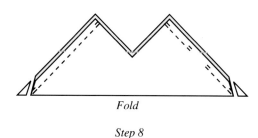

Fold

Step 8

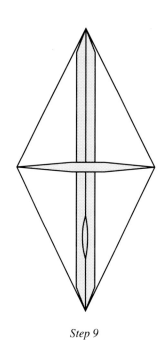

Step 9

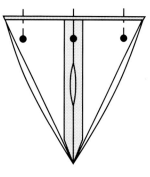

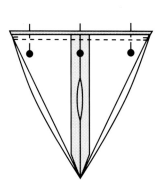

Step 10   *Step 11*

Made by Margaret Stephenson Coole, copyright © 1984. Collection of Robert and Ardis James.

Night Shades: A variety of blue and white print fabrics are used for the background units. They are arranged in a light to dark value sequence. A variety of window fabrics are used. I suggest that you experiment with color placement to achieve a pleasing pattern. The exact amounts you will need of each fabric will depend upon your creative decisions. For added interest, Margaret has sewn star-shaped sequins and beads at the intersections of the windows.

SPECTROSCOPE

Made by Margaret Stephenson Coole, copyright © 1990/VIS∗ART Copyright, Inc.

Spectroscope: One background fabric is used. The windows are arranged in a reverse color progression.

NIGHT SHADES
AND SPECTROSCOPE

Finished unit: 3¾″ square	WALL	TWIN	DOUBLE/QUEEN	KING
Finished size	37½″ × 37½″	71″ × 90″	86″ × 86″	97½″ × 97½″
Units set	10 × 10	19 × 24	23 × 23	26 × 26
Total units	100	456	529	676

FABRIC NEEDED (YARDS)

Background - total amount	4½	21	24	31
Windows - total amount	¾	3½	4	5

CUTTING YOUR FABRIC

Use Templates A and C.

	WALL	TWIN	DOUBLE/QUEEN	KING
Background: Template C, number of 8″ squares	100	456	529	676
Windows: Template A	180	869	1012	1300

If you would like to use quick-cutting techniques, you can cut 2¼″ squares and then cut a slight curve in each side (as shown on the template pattern) when you are inserting the windows.

PUTTING IT ALL TOGETHER

1. Make the required number of square units from the background fabric. Refer to Steps 1-17 of "Square Units" for help.

2. Join the square units and insert the window fabrics to complete the quilt. Refer to Steps 18-25 of "Square Units" for help.

NIGHTFALL DIAMONDS

Hand pieced by Ethel Selberg and Laura Nownes. Color arrangement by Bill Folk.

Raffle quilt made by the Osage County Artists and Craftsmen. Collection of Isabelle Lynch.
Courtesy of Vickie McKenney, The Calico Basket, Edmonds, Washington.

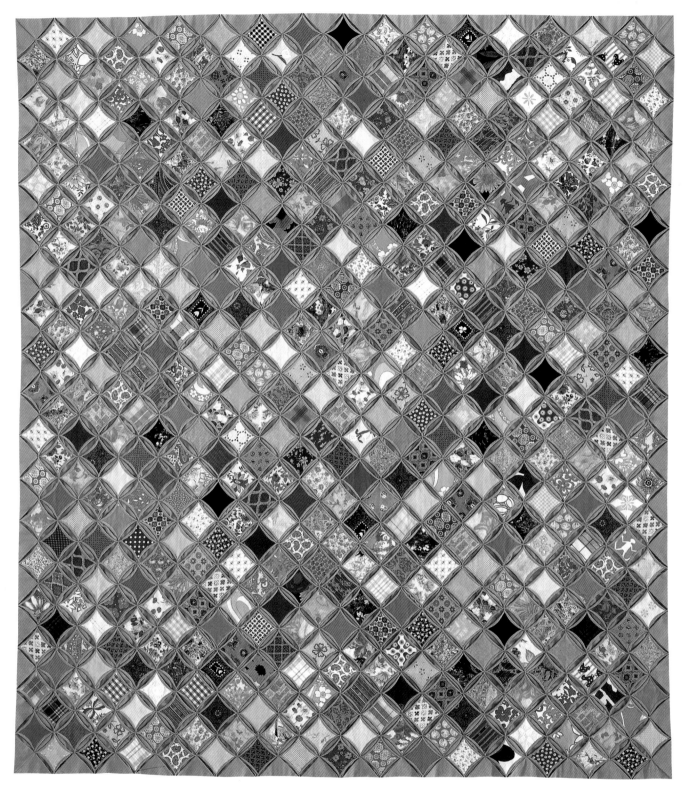

Hand pieced by Adele Ingraham.

NIGHTFALL DIAMONDS, TRADITIONAL AND EVERY PANE A MEMORY

Finished unit: 4″ square	WALL	TWIN	DOUBLE/QUEEN	KING
Finished size	40″ × 40″	72″ × 88″	88″ × 88″	100″ × 100″
Units set	10 × 10	18 × 22	22 × 22	25 × 25
Total units	100	396	484	625
FABRIC NEEDED (YARDS)				
Background	5	19	23	30
Windows: fabric total	1	3½	4	5¼
CUTTING YOUR FABRIC				
Use Templates B and D.				
Background: Template D, number of 8½″ squares	100	396	484	625
Windows: Template B	180	752	924	1200

If you would like to use quick-cutting techniques, you can cut 2½″ squares and then cut a slight curve in each side (as shown on the template pattern) when you are inserting the windows.

PUTTING IT ALL TOGETHER

1. Make the required number of square units from the background fabric. Refer to Steps 1-17 of "Square Units" for help.

2. Join the square units and insert the window fabric to complete the quilt. Refer to Steps 18-25 of "Square Units" for help.

QUADRIANCE

Made by Margaret Stephenson Coole, copyright © 1990/VIS∗ART Copyright Inc.

This quilt combines three sizes of square units and three sizes of rectangular units.

Finished sizes of units:

2″ square

4″ square

7½″ square

2″ × 4″ rectangle

2″ × 7½″ rectangle

4″ × 7½″ rectangle

Finished size	$37'' \times 37''$
Units set	9×9
Total number of units	81

FABRIC NEEDED (YARDS)

Background	$6\frac{1}{2}$
Windows - total amount	$1\frac{3}{4}$

CUTTING YOUR FABRIC

Use Templates D, F, G, H, I, J, K, L, M, N, O and P.

Background:

For square units: Template F, number of $4\frac{1}{2}''$ squares	9
Template D, number of $8\frac{1}{2}''$ squares	16
Template G, number of $15\frac{1}{2}''$ squares	4
For rectangular units: Template N	24
Template O	12
Template P	16
Windows: Template H	24
Template I	16
Template J	24
Template K	16
Template L	32
Template M	32

Placement of background units

F	N	O	N	F	N	O	N	F
N	D	P	D	N	D	P	D	N
O	P	G	P	O	P	G	P	O
N	D	P	D	N	D	P	D	N
F	N	O	N	F	N	O	N	F
N	D	P	D	N	D	P	D	N
O	P	G	P	O	P	G	P	O
N	D	P	D	N	D	P	D	N
F	N	O	N	F	N	O	N	F

PUTTING IT ALL TOGETHER

1. Make the required number of square units from background fabric. Refer to Steps 1-17 of "Square Units" for help.

2. Make the required number of rectangular units from background fabric. Refer to Steps 1-11 of "Rectangular Units" for help.

3. Join the units, referring to the illustration for the exact placement.

4. Insert the window fabrics, referring to the illustration for the exact placement, then finish with Step 12.

I suggest that you experiment with color placement to achieve a pleasing pattern.

Template patterns are given for the various sizes of diamond-shaped windows. You may find it easier to cut a piece of fabric larger than the space, put it in place and then trim it to fit the space (about $\frac{1}{4}''$ smaller all around), as shown on the template patterns. However, be *very* careful that you *do not cut into the background fabric.*

Placement of window pieces

ARMCHAIR CADDY

Made by Laura Nownes.

This project requires only four 3¾″ finished *Cathedral Window* squares. Make it to hang over your chair to keep your sewing supplies handy.

Finished size	9½″ × 21½″
Square size	3¾″

FABRIC NEEDED (YARDS)

Blue	1
Floral	½
Pink (windows)	⅛
Green (accent)	¼
Batting	⅜

CUTTING YOUR FABRIC

Use Templates A, C and E.

Blue fabric: Template C, number of 8″ squares	4
10″ squares (pocket linings)	2
10″ × 22″ rectangle (backing)	1
6″ × 10″ rectangle (pincushion)	1
3¼″ × 9½″ rectangles (binding)	4
3¼″ × 22½″ rectangles (binding)	2
Floral fabric: 10″ squares (outer pockets)	2
10″ × 22″ rectangle (body)	1
Window fabric: Template A	4
Accent fabric: Template E, 4¼″ squares	4
Batting: 10″ squares (pockets)	2
10″ × 22″ rectangle (body)	1

1. To make the *Cathedral Window* unit: Stitch and fold the four 8″ squares of blue fabric as instructed in Steps 1-17 of "Square Units."

2. Join the units together to make two units across by two units down.

3. Insert the four pieces of accent fabric. See the instructions in "Variation" for help.

4. Insert the window pieces. See Steps 23-25 of "Square Units" for help.

5. Set the completed *Cathedral Window* unit aside until you are ready to attach it to the pocket unit of the caddy.

6. With their right sides facing out, sandwich the large piece of batting between the 10″ × 22″ pieces of blue and floral pieces.

7. Hand or machine quilt the layers together. The sample has been sewn in a 1½″ diagonal grid.

8. Even the edges and trim to measure 9½″ × 21½″.

9. Using the 10″ squares of blue fabric, floral fabric and batting, layer and stitch them as you did in Steps 6 and 7 to make two pocket units.

10. Even the edges and trim the pockets to measure 9½″ square.

11. Use a 3¼″ × 9½″ piece of blue fabric to bind one edge on each pocket.

12. Lay the body of the caddy on a flat surface, with the right side facing up.

13. With their right sides facing up, position the two pockets at opposite ends of the caddy.

14. With its wrong side facing out, fold the blue 6″ × 10″ pincushion piece in half lengthwise. Stitch along the length with a ¼″ seam.

15. Turn this piece right side out. Position the seam at the center of one side and then stitch one end closed ½″ from the edge.

16. Fill the pincushion with birdseed. Stitch the opposite end closed.

17. With the seamed side down, position the pincushion across the center of the caddy. Stitch it in place along each side. Trim any excess fabric.

18. Use two 3¼″ × 9½″ pieces of blue fabric to bind the two ends of the caddy with a ½″ finished binding.

19. Use the two 3¼″ × 22½″ pieces to bind the two lengths of the caddy, turning in ½″ at each end.

20. Center the *Cathedral Window* section over one of the pockets and pin it in place.

21. Hand stitch this unit to the pocket, stitching only on the sides and bottom edges, leaving the top loose to create a pocket. Be careful to stitch only through the top layer of the pocket unit.

22. This completes your armchair caddy.

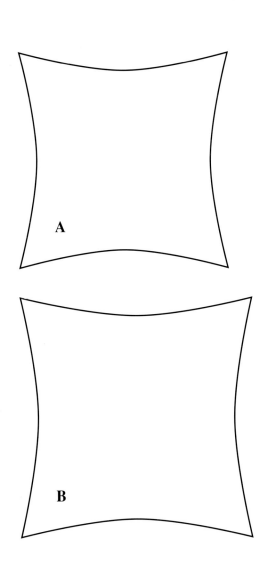

A

B

Fold

C

D

E

F

G

Fold

Fold

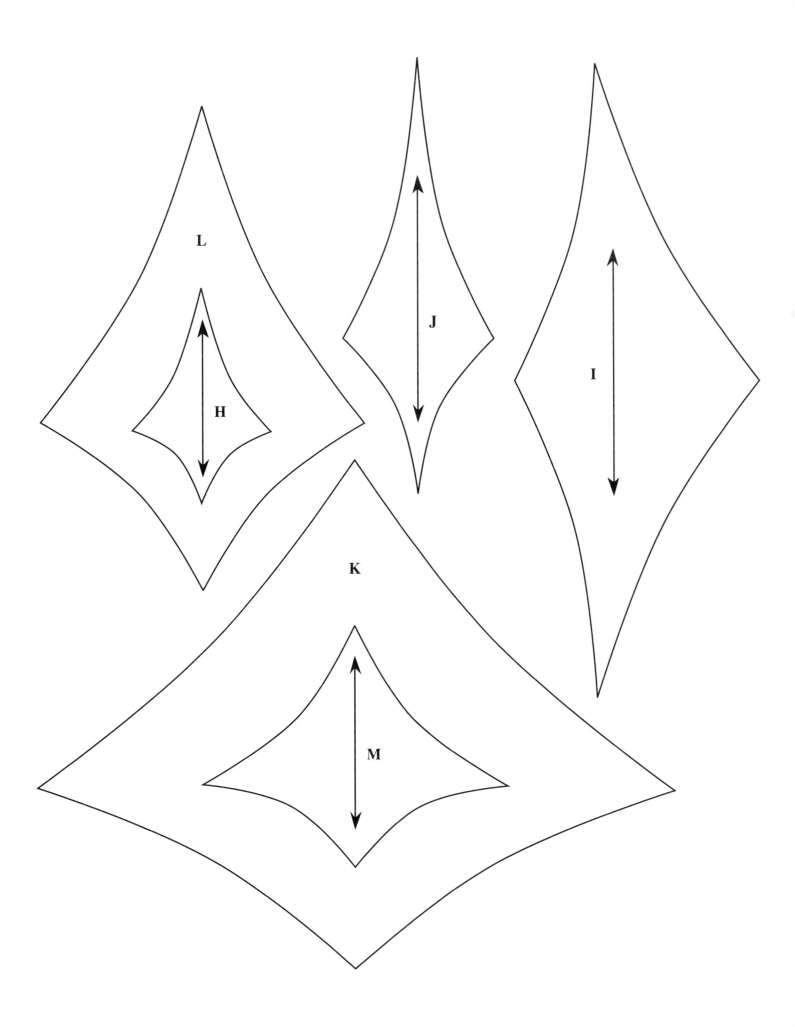

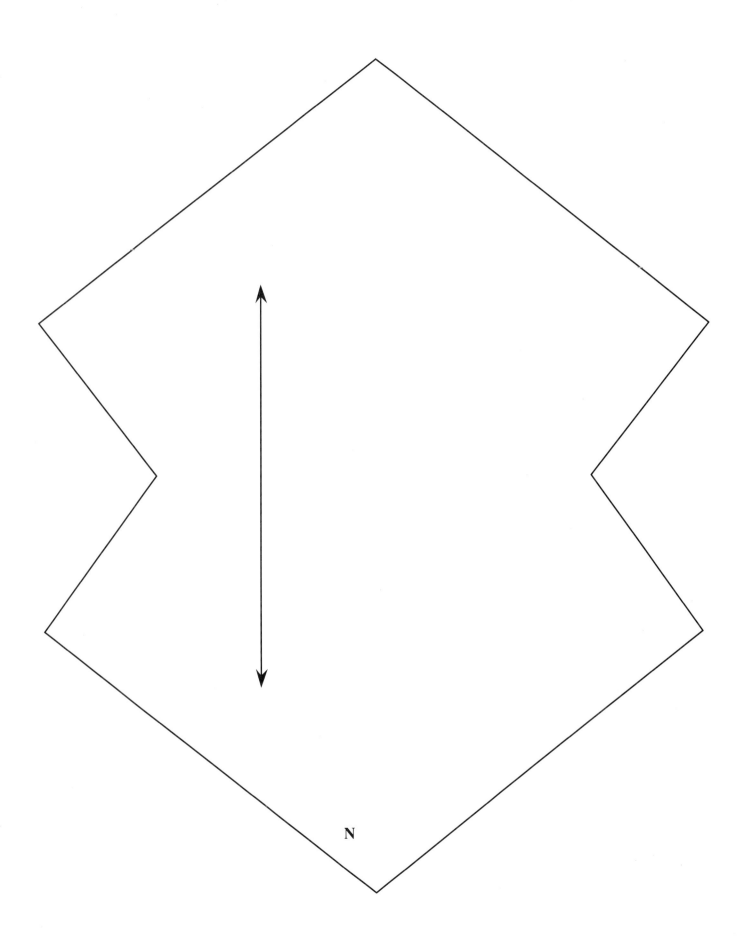

N

One-quarter of pattern

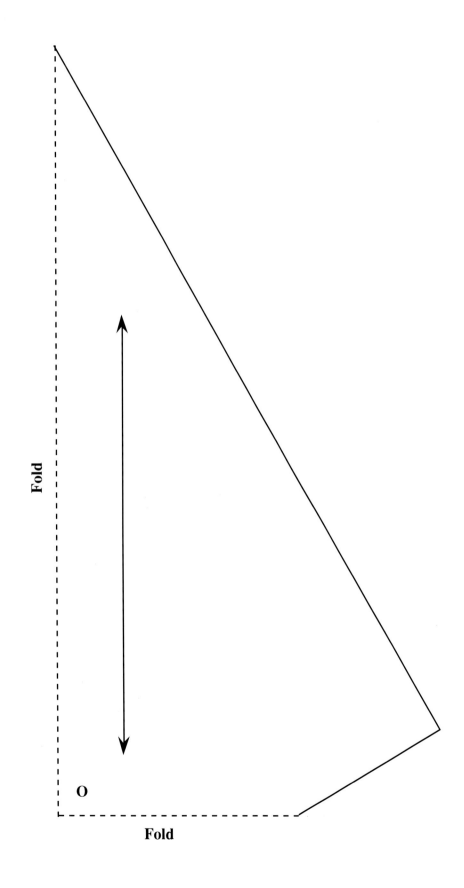

Fold

O

Fold

One-quarter of pattern

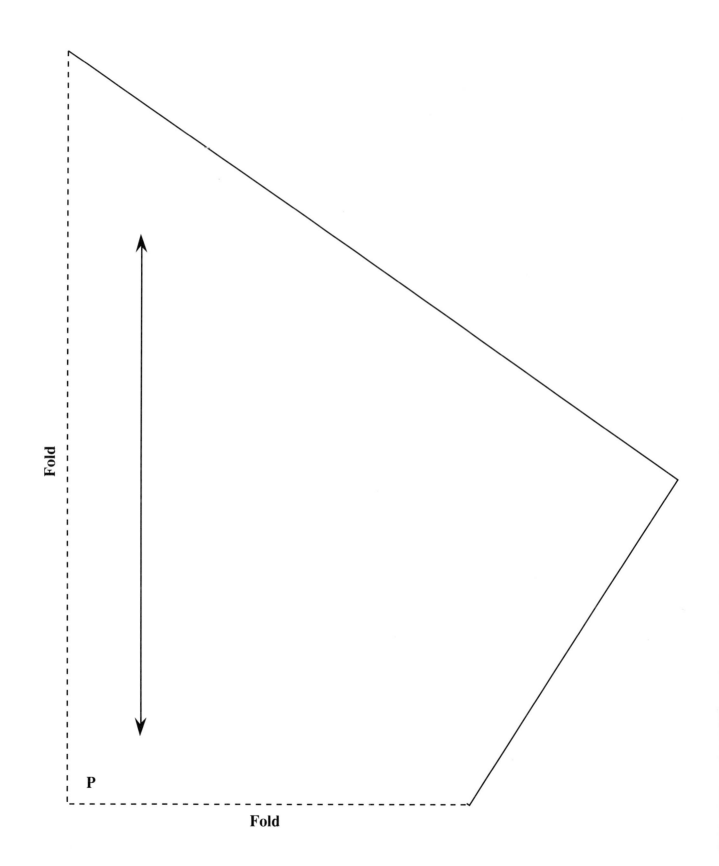

Fold

P

Fold

Simply the Best

*W*hen we started our publishing efforts in 1983, we made one pledge to ourselves: to produce the finest quilt books imaginable. The critics and our loyal readers clearly believe that we're living up to that promise.

In a time when thin, 64-page quilt books with only staples to hold their pages intact and small numbers of color photos sell for as much as $19.95, we are proud that our books set a noticeably higher standard.

Books from The Quilt Digest Press are hefty, with many more pages and masses of color photos. They are printed on high-quality satin-finish paper and are bound with durable glues and spines to last a lifetime. The world's finest quilt photographer does all our work. A great design team lavishes its attention on every detail of every page. And the world's finest commercial printer sees to it that every book is a gem. Add knowledgeable authors with vital ideas and you, too, will say, "The Quilt Digest Press? Oh, they're Simply the Best."

Try another of our books. They're as good as the one in your hands. And write for our free color catalogue.

THE QUILT DIGEST PRESS

Dept. D
P.O. Box 1331
Gualala, CA 95445